EARTH SCIENCE LIBRARY

WEATHER

MARTYN BRAMWELL

Updated Edition

Franklin Watts

New York · Chicago · London · Toronto · Sydney

Second Edition
© 1987, 1994 by
Franklin Watts
All rights reserved

Franklin Watts

Library of Congress
Cataloging-in-Publication Data
Bramwell, Martyn.
Weather / by Martyn Bramwell. –
Rev. ed.
p. cm. – (Earth science library)
Includes index.
ISBN 0–531–14306–6
1. Weather – Juvenile literature.
2. Meteorology – Juvenile literature.
[1. Weather. 2. Meteorology.] I. Title.
II. Series: Bramwell, Martyn. Earth
science library.
QC863.5.B73 1994
551.5. — dc20   93–42016
                            CIP   AC

Printed in Belgium

Designed by Ben White

Picture research by Mick
Alexander

Illustrations:
Chris Forsey
Hayward Art Group

Photographs:
Ardea 18*l*, 29
British Antarctic Survey 24
Bruce Coleman 9, 18*r*, 21*r*
Daily Telegraph Colour Library 5*l*
ESA 25*r*
GeoScience Features 28
Robert Harding 1, 16
David Hosking 7
Frank Lane 11, 15, 17*r*, 21*l*, 23
Meteorological Office 13
Mountain Camera 5*r*
Science Photo Library 14, 25*l*, 26,
   27
Seaphot 19*r*
ZEFA 10, 17*l*, 19*l*, 20, 22

EARTH SCIENCE LIBRARY

WEATHER

Contents

The atmosphere

Everything we call "weather," from the still, calm days of summer to the most violent storms of winter, happens in the bottom-most layer of the **atmosphere** – the thin layer of gases that surrounds the Earth. Clouds, rain, wind, and heat waves are all produced by the heating, cooling and constant churning of this thin gas layer.

There are traces of atmosphere up to 600 miles (1,000 km) out into space, but because of the pull of **gravity**, most of the gas is squashed into a thin layer close to the Earth's surface. In fact, three-quarters of the atmosphere is compressed into a layer, called the troposphere, which is between 6 and 10 miles (10–16 km) thick.

▽ The diameter of the Earth is about 12,750 km (7,920 miles). The atmosphere around it is about 10 km (6 miles) thick. Compared to the size of the Earth, this life-giving layer of gas is about as thick as a layer of varnish covering a schoolroom globe!

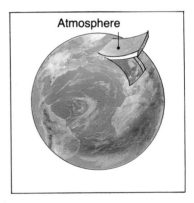

Atmosphere

◁ The lowest layer of the atmosphere is called the *troposphere*, and this is where all our weather is made. Above it lies a much thicker layer called the *stratosphere*. Here the air is already far too thin to breathe. It is also very cold. At 10 km (6 miles) high, the air temperature is −60°C (−76°F). Higher still there are other layers, in which the air gets thinner and thinner until it merges eventually with outer space.

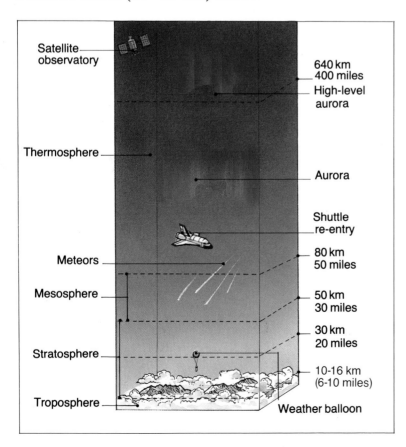

Satellite observatory

Thermosphere

Meteors

Mesosphere

Stratosphere

Troposphere

640 km / 400 miles
High-level aurora

Aurora

Shuttle re-entry

80 km / 50 miles

50 km / 30 miles

30 km / 20 miles

10-16 km (6-10 miles)

Weather balloon

◁ Sunlight reflecting off the atmosphere, clouds and oceans gives Earth its characteristic blue color when viewed from space. When the planet is lit from a low angle like this, the atmosphere shines like a thin blue-white halo.

The atmosphere is actually a mixture of gases. Nearly four-fifths is nitrogen, and most of the rest is oxygen, along with small amounts of water vapor, carbon dioxide and several other gases.

Most of the gases came originally from inside the Earth, blasted out of volcanoes millions of years ago when the Earth was young. But Earth's original atmosphere was very different from ours today. It was poisonous, with hardly any oxygen. The life-giving oxygen came later, once plants had appeared. Plants use sunlight and carbon dioxide to grow, and they produce oxygen in the process. So we owe our breathable atmosphere to the simple plants that evolved on Earth millions of years in the past.

But today's atmosphere does more than just provide the oxygen we need. It acts like a blanket around the Earth. Without it we would fry during the day and freeze at night. It also filters out harmful ultraviolet radiation from the Sun. And in its lowest layers it contains water, which not only supports life but also makes the clouds – and the rain, hail and snow that falls from them.

△ The higher you go, the less oxygen there is in the air. That is why many people feel lightheaded or dizzy if they go above 3,000 m (9,800 ft). At 6,000 m (19,700 ft) even the fittest mountaineers may suffer from mountain sickness, so oxygen masks are often worn for the final attack on the summit.

The weather machine

All weather systems need energy to drive their swirling movements over the face of the Earth. That energy comes from the distant Sun. To understand how weather works, we must first look at the way the Sun heats the Earth's surface.

Because the Earth's surface is curved, the Sun's rays are concentrated near the equator but more spread out near the poles. This uneven heating effect is the first stage in setting up the energy "machine" that drives our weather.

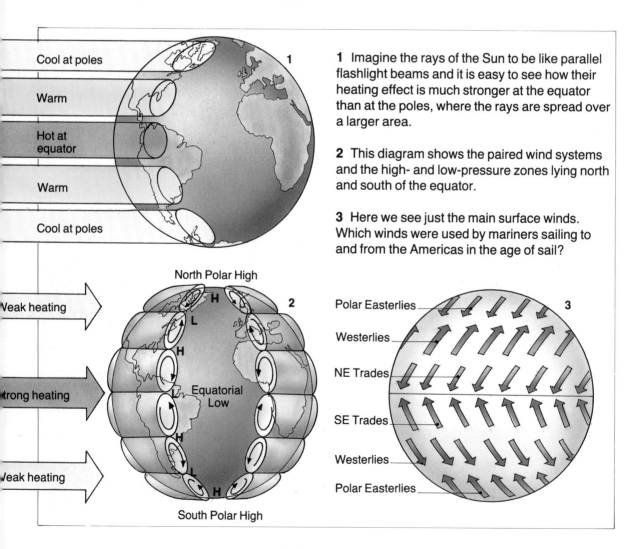

Cool at poles
Warm
Hot at equator
Warm
Cool at poles

Weak heating
Strong heating
Weak heating

North Polar High
Equatorial Low
South Polar High

Polar Easterlies
Westerlies
NE Trades
SE Trades
Westerlies
Polar Easterlies

1 Imagine the rays of the Sun to be like parallel flashlight beams and it is easy to see how their heating effect is much stronger at the equator than at the poles, where the rays are spread over a larger area.

2 This diagram shows the paired wind systems and the high- and low-pressure zones lying north and south of the equator.

3 Here we see just the main surface winds. Which winds were used by mariners sailing to and from the Americas in the age of sail?

Warm air is lighter than cool air, so it tends to rise. Cold air is heavy, and so it sinks. The strong heating effect near the equator makes the air in that region rise. As the air rises upward, away from the surface, the pressure at the surface is reduced. This produces a low-pressure zone near the equator.

Higher in the atmosphere, the air spreads out north and south of the equator. It then cools and sinks again. The result is a matching pair of zones of sinking air. As the air presses down on the surface, it produces zones of high pressure.

Finally, because the wind always blows from high pressure to low, the air flows back toward the equator. The result is the two sets of winds we call the Trade Winds. Similar wind systems in the **temperate** regions produce the Westerlies, and in the far north and south a third pair gives us the Polar Easterlies.

The seasons, mountain ranges and the pattern of land and sea all produce variations, but these main winds are the "conveyor belts" that carry our weather systems around the world.

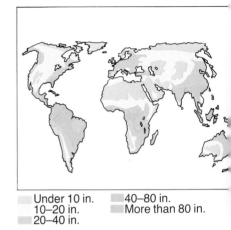

Under 10 in.
10–20 in.
20–40 in.
40–80 in.
More than 80 in.

△ The western sides of Europe and North America receive plenty of rain, carried in by the Westerly winds. The Trade Winds carry rain into the Amazon jungle. But see how deserts often lie downwind of mountain ranges. By the time the air gets there, it has lost all its moisture over the high ground.

▷ Rainfall is very unevenly distributed over the Earth's surface. Large parts of the African, Asian and South American rainforests have more than 500 cm (200 in) of rain a year, while some parts of the Atacama Desert in Chile have never seen a single drop.

What makes the wind blow?

If you blow into a balloon and then let go of the neck, the air immediately rushes out again with a loud spluttering sound. The reason is that the air in the balloon has been forced in under pressure. As soon as it can, the air rushes from the high-pressure area inside the balloon to the low-pressure area outside. The air will keep on flowing out until the pressure inside the balloon is the same as the pressure outside.

On a much bigger scale, this is what makes the wind blow. Whenever there is a difference in air pressure between two places on the Earth's surface, the wind will try to even things up by blowing from high to low. And the bigger the difference in pressure between the two areas, the harder the wind will blow.

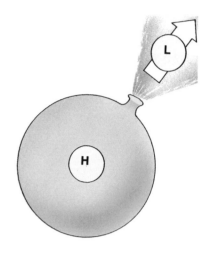

△ The balloon experiment is a simple way of demonstrating how air will always move from a high-pressure area to one of low pressure.

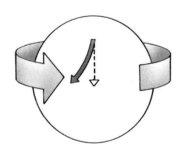

△ The Earth's spin affects winds, currents and anything else that is free to move over the surface. In the case of wind, the air *tries* to flow straight from the high-pressure area to the Low at the equator. At the same time, the Earth is turning, so the path the wind traces on the surface is actually a sweeping curve.

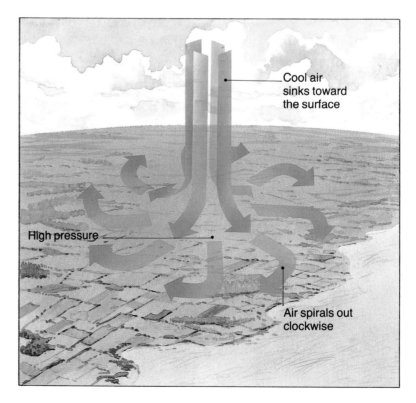

Cool air sinks toward the surface

High pressure

Air spirals out clockwise

From this we would expect all the winds on the Earth's surface to blow straight from high-pressure areas to low-pressure areas.

But, things are not quite as simple. Because the Earth is spinning, the winds are pushed off course – to the right of their expected path in the northern hemisphere and to the left in the southern hemisphere. That is why the Trade Winds, Westerlies and Polar Easterlies blow across the face of the Earth at an angle, instead of simply blowing north or south from the high-pressure zones to low-pressure zones.

The same thing happens in smaller-scale Highs and Lows. Instead of blowing straight out from a High, the winds spiral outward – clockwise in the northern hemisphere and counterclockwise in the southern. Winds moving inward toward a Low also spiral – but in the opposite direction.

△Dust devils are smallscale desert whirlwinds caused by very hot air rising upward from the Sun-scorched surface.

◁The drawing on the left gives a three-dimensional view of how the air moves in a high-pressure system in the northern winter. Heavy cool air sinks down toward the surface and then spirals outward.

▷The illustration on the right gives a similar view of a northern hemisphere low-pressure system, also called a **depression**. The warm air is drawn inward, and then rises, spreading out again at high level.

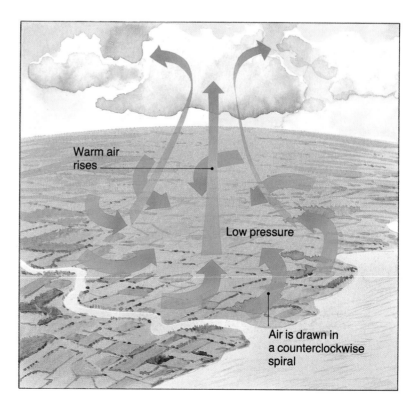

Warm air rises

Low pressure

Air is drawn in a counterclockwise spiral

How do clouds form?

Although we take water for granted, it is really a very special substance that exists on Earth quite naturally in three quite different forms – liquid, solid ice and invisible gas. The invisible gas is called water vapor. It is always present in the air around us, and the warmer the air is, the more water vapor it can hold. Our breath, for example, is very moist. On a warm day there is no way of knowing this. But breathe out on a cold day and a small cloud forms in front of your face. That cloud is made of millions of minute droplets of water. They have **condensed**, that is, turned from invisible gas into droplets of liquid, because the cold air could not hold all the water vapor.

△ Moisture in the air will condense on the outside of a very cold glass. The same thing happens when you breathe on a cold window – a mist of droplets forms.

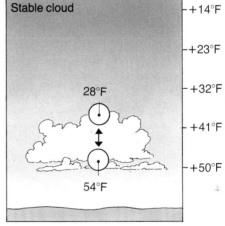

Stable cloud

+14°F
+23°F
28°F — +32°F
— +41°F
— +50°F
54°F

Small "fair weather" clouds are typical of high-pressure conditions in summer. The air is descending gently and is said to be stable. The air at the top of the cloud is no warmer than the air around it, and the cloud does not get any bigger.

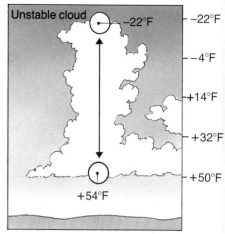

The rising air in a low-pressure system is usually unstable. It is warmer than its surroundings and rises like a bubble to produce towering storm clouds.

Clouds in the sky form in just the same way. As long as the air can cope with the water vapor in it, the sky remains clear. But as soon as the air is **saturated**, that is, holding as much water as it can at that temperature, any extra moisture will condense into droplets – and clouds will form.

This is why, even on a clear day, there are often clouds over hills. As the breeze carries the air over the hill, it is forced higher. The higher it goes, the colder it gets. As the air cools, it can no longer hold as much water vapor, and so a patch of cloud forms.

Clouds provide many useful weather clues. Small, fluffy *cumulus* clouds indicate fine settled weather, but big towering *cumulus* clouds often grow into *cumulonimbus* storm clouds, with thunder, lightning and rain. High, wispy *cirrus* clouds are often followed by lower layers of flat *stratus*, and then by very low, dark, *nimbostratus* rain clouds.

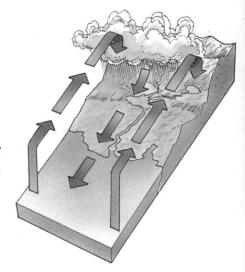

△ Warm air flowing over the sea absorbs moisture and carries it inland. As the air rises over hills, the water condenses into clouds, then falls to Earth as rain. Rivers carry it back to the sea – and the process starts all over again.

11

Weather on the move

▽ A depression usually starts as a kink in the boundary between masses of warm and cold air. As the kink gets bigger, the air takes on a turning motion. Cold air moves in behind the trapped sector of warm air – pushing it along and also pushing beneath it like a wedge.

For much of the year, the weather in the temperate regions of the world is controlled by depressions. These are low-pressure weather systems that sweep in from the west carrying rain and snow, blustery winds and low temperatures. Unlike the high-pressure systems that bring the hot, dry, still days of summer, and often stay around for days – or weeks – at a time, depressions are very active. They move quickly, often arriving one after another in "families."

Most of these Lows start life far out in the Atlantic and Pacific oceans, in the northern parts of those oceans where two great masses of air meet. To the north lies the cold, heavy Arctic air mass. To the south lie the warmer, wetter, Atlantic and Pacific air masses. The boundary between them is called the Polar Front.

An Atlantic depression

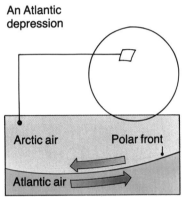

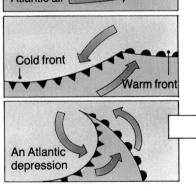

Condensation level: the flat cloud base shows the level at which water vapor condenses.

Thunderstorms, rain and hail often accompany a cold front.

Cold front: Clear, cooler weather often follows the passing of a cold front.

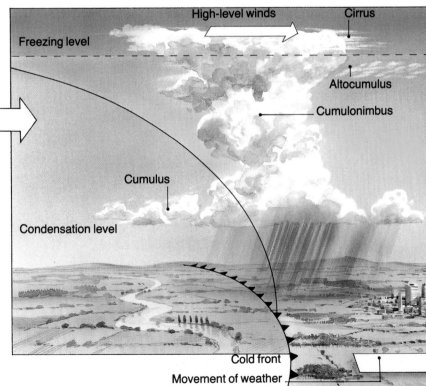

The depression starts as a small kink on this **front**. As the air moves eastward across the ocean, carried along by the westerly winds, the kink becomes more pronounced. It takes on a distinctive upside-down V-shape that traps a triangular wedge of warm, moist, air between two huge masses of colder air. The kink has now become two fronts – a warm front marking the leading edge of the warm air, and a cold front that marks the edge of the cold air behind it.

Gradually the cold air pushes underneath the warm air, forcing it upward. This creates an area of low pressure. As the warm, moist air rises, it produces a whole series of different cloud types, each one associated with a different part of the frontal system.

The diagram below shows the sequence of clouds and weather that accompanies a depression as it passes across the landscape.

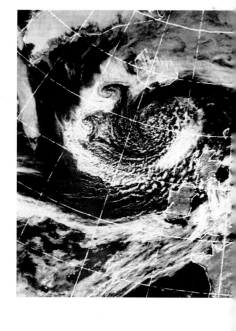

△ This satellite photograph shows the broad, curving bands of cloud created by a frontal system centered on a Low near Iceland.

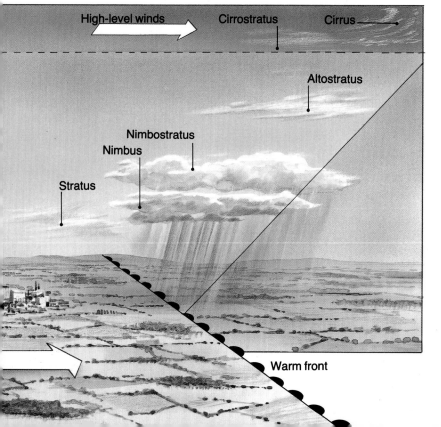

High-level winds · Cirrostratus · Cirrus

Altostratus

Nimbostratus

Nimbus

Stratus

Warm front

The first signs: the approach of a warm front is often indicated by wispy cirrus clouds. Because they are so high they are made of ice crystals, not water droplets.

Warm sector: as the warm air is forced upward it cools. As it cools, its moisture condenses into clouds.

Layer clouds: as the front moves in, the sky is filled with layer upon layer of flat gray rain clouds.

The warm front is usually flatter and less steep than the rounded, bulbous front of the cold air mass.

13

Clouds out of control

Hurricanes, or typhoons as they are known in China and Japan, are among the most violent storms. They occur most frequently in tropical regions, over the warm seas of the western Atlantic, Pacific and Indian oceans. They probably start as perfectly ordinary Lows like the ones that sweep into Europe from the Atlantic. But for some reason they grow – and grow.

We still do not know exactly what makes a hurricane develop, but fueled by a plentiful supply of its two main requirements – warmth and moisture – a small storm system can rapidly grow into a mature hurricane. It can be 600 km (370 miles) across, with walls of cloud 15 km (9 miles) high and winds of 160 km/h (100 mph). Occasionally a real monster develops. Typhoon Tip, which roared across the western Pacific in 1979, was more than 2,200 km (1,370 miles) in diameter and had winds of 300 km/h (190 mph).

△ This satellite photograph, taken on August 8, 1980, shows the huge spiral swirl and central eye of Hurricane Allen filling the Gulf of Mexico. A smaller un-named hurricane can be seen developing off the west coast of Mexico.

A typical hurricane

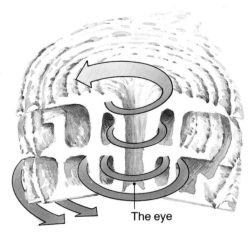

The eye

◁Smashed houses and uprooted trees mark the path of a hurricane. In the United States alone, hurricanes cause billions of dollars' worth of damage every year. Hurricane Andrew in 1992 hit the Bahamas and the Southeast, causing damage estimated at $15 billion.

△Although similar to a hurricane, a tornado packs all its destructive energy into a column of rotating cloud several feet to over a mile in diameter. Wind speeds may exceed 320 km/h (200 mph), and the winds around the low-pressure eye are strong enough to pick up cattle and parts of buildings. Tornadoes are most common in Kansas and Oklahoma, where warm, damp air from the Gulf of Mexico meets cold air from the Rockies.

As long as a hurricane remains at sea it is a danger only to shipping. But several times each year, hurricanes tear into the Atlantic coast of the southern United States, low-lying coastal regions of the Bay of Bengal, and the islands and mainland coasts of the western Pacific. The effects are devastating. Forests and plantations are knocked down or torn from the ground. Crops are demolished by the wind and torrential rain. Vast areas are flooded, and buildings are demolished. In 1970 almost a million people died when a huge storm hit the heavily populated Ganges Delta in Bangladesh. Most died in floods that followed the storm.

But once the storm has moved on to land it is doomed. Without the warm tropical ocean to feed its huge appetite for heat energy and moisture, it starts to die. The winds slacken, the cloud bands break up, and the low-pressure "eye" fills in.

Snow, rain and hail

The tiny droplets of water that make up clouds are so small that it takes about a million of them to make one raindrop. And yet everything we call **precipitation** – rain, hail, snow, **sleet** or **drizzle** – starts off as this mist of microscopic water droplets.

Rain is thought to form in two ways. In the temperate parts of the world, clouds often extend upward into regions where the temperature is well below freezing. Here, the droplets turn to ice crystals, and as they drift downward they first grow into snowflakes. Then, as they meet warmer air, they melt and fall as rain.

In the warm clouds of the tropical regions, water droplets floating in the air collide and merge together. Frequent collisions produce bigger and bigger drops until finally the raindrops are heavy enough to fall to Earth.

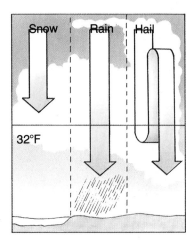

△The diagram above shows how the three main types of precipitation are formed. Rain and snow form in the same way – but whether the water reaches the ground as a raindrop or snowflake depends on the temperature of the air between the cloud and the ground. If the air temperature is around 4°C (39°F), we are likely to get a mixture of rain, snow and partly melted snowflakes. This is what we call sleet. Drizzle is very fine rain with raindrops less than half a millimeter across. It usually falls from low stratus clouds.

◁Thick snow may look very pretty, but in large cities it will also bring congestion as roads are blocked, water pipes are frozen, and telephone lines are brought down by the weight of the snow on them.

◁In winter, the main winds over Asia blow outward from a high-pressure area in Siberia. In summer the winds are reversed. A low-pressure area in northwest India draws moist air in over the Indian Ocean, bringing the torrential rains of the **monsoon** season.

Snow forms when tiny droplets of water freeze into ice crystals and then grow into more complex snowflakes as more crystals freeze on to them. As the flakes get heavier, they fall under the pull of gravity, and as long as the air temperature at ground level is below 4°C (39°F) the flakes will remain frozen and cover the ground with a carpet of snow.

The air currents inside a large cumulonimbus thundercloud rise and fall in a constant churning motion. Water droplets are carried high into the freezing level, then fall again. But instead of falling to Earth, they get swept back up again. Each time they pass above the freezing level another layer of ice is added to the frozen raindrop.

Eventually the ball of ice becomes so heavy that it plunges through the base of the cloud and plummets to Earth as a hailstone.

△Hailstones can cause enormous damage to crops, and the biggest stones – up to the size of baseballs – can damage buildings and cars and kill animals as big as cattle and sheep. The largest hailstone on record fell at Coffeyville, Kansas, in 1970. It was 19 cm (7½ in) in diameter.

Dew, frost, mist and fog

Anyone who has ever spent a night in a tent will know the sodden grass and wet canvas that greet the early riser. The city dweller, too, will be familiar with the layer of water drops on the roofs of cars in the morning. In neither case has it rained. The water has simply condensed out of the air as dew. As the temperature falls during the night, especially on clear nights when there is no blanket of cloud to trap the Earth's warmth, the air quickly cools to the point at which it can no longer hold all the water vapor in it. That temperature is called the **dew point**, and as soon as it is reached the excess moisture in the air condenses into drops of liquid.

If the dew point is below 0°C (32°F), the water vapor condenses in the form of ice crystals, covering everything with glistening hoarfrost.

▽ Hoarfrost is often the sign of a cold night with little or no cloud. But the frost is usually short-lived: the ice crystals quickly melt as the morning Sun warms the air.

◁ Dew is most common in autumn and winter when the air is cool and damp. In summer the nights are often too short for the temperature to fall to the dew point.

Fog and mist are really just cloud at ground level. The only difference lies in the way they form. While cloud forms when moist air rises and cools, fog forms when air cools near the ground. This often happens at night, and is common over damp ground like riverside meadows.

In mountain regions, night fog is common. The air is cold and heavy and so it sinks to the valley bottom, producing fog which may last well into the day, even when the hills are in sunshine.

Freezing fog consists of water droplets that are actually *below* 0°C (32°F). They are called **super-cooled** droplets, and they can remain liquid while they drift in the air but immediately turn to ice crystals when they touch a cold surface.

▽Trees and hills rise like islands from a sea of early morning fog. During the night the low-lying ground has cooled, and the air above it has cooled in turn, releasing some of its water vapor in a mist of microscopic droplets.

△Smog may be a mixture of fog and the smoke and dust from industrial cities. An even nastier type of smog is **photo-chemical** smog like this in Los Angeles, formed by the action of sunlight on the fumes from car exhausts.

Lights in the sky

For thousands of years people have wondered at the strange and beautiful lights that appear in the sky from time to time.

Some of the most spectacular are the lights of the **aurora** – seen most frequently in the polar regions. They are caused by electrically charged particles from the Sun becoming trapped in the Earth's **magnetic field**. High above the Earth these particles pass some of their energy to gas **molecules** in the upper atmosphere, causing them to flicker and glow with an eerie light.

Closer to Earth, the most familiar of nature's special effects is the rainbow. As the Sun's rays strike a raindrop, most of the light passes straight through, but rays catching the edge of the drop are bent inward. They are then reflected off the back of the raindrop and out again. But on the way the **white light** of the Sun is split into the colors of the rainbow.

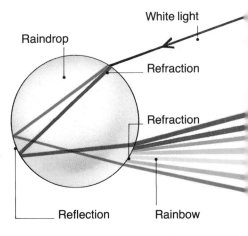

△Sunlight striking the edge of the raindrop is refracted, or bent, toward the interior of the drop. But white light is really a mixture of light of many different colors (that is, different **wavelengths**) and each color is bent by a different amount. As a result the colors are separated. They are then reflected off the back of the raindrop – and are separated even more as they leave the drop. The result is an arc of color: blue on the inside, and red on the outside.

◁A perfect rainbow over the flat marshlands of the Camargue in southern France. Occasionally you may see a double rainbow – one "normal" bow with another, paler, bow outside it with the colors in reverse order.

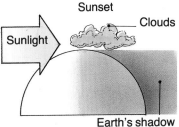

△Sunsets are caused by the rays of the Sun lighting up the clouds from underneath, even when, to an observer at ground level, the Sun has long since sunk below the horizon.

△A beautiful display of halo, Sun dogs, pillars and arcs, photographed through a fine layer of ice-crystal cirrus cloud in Antarctica.

Halos are also caused by **refraction** (bending) and **reflection** of light, by tiny ice crystals in the air. They are often seen when there is a thin veil of cirrus cloud over the Sun. When the Sun is low in the sky, the halo may be accompanied by a Sun pillar, a column of light from the Sun down to the horizon; by mock Suns, or Sun dogs, which are bright patches on the halo, level with the Sun; or by partial halos which touch the main halo at the top and sides.

The lunar corona is a night-time display worth watching for. It appears as a deep blue ring around the Moon, often with a red outer edge. It is best seen through thin cloud, and is caused by the water droplets that make up the cloud.

Thunder and lightning

If you run a plastic comb very quickly several times through dry hair, you will build up a charge of **static electricity** on the comb. It will make a crackling sound, and may even give off a spark. That, on a colossal scale, is how lightning is produced. In the violent air currents inside a thundercloud, ice crystals, hailstones and water droplets of all sizes are tossed up and down, rubbing against each other until enormous charges of static electricity are built up in different parts of the cloud.

Eventually, when the charges reach several million volts, the air can no longer hold them. They are discharged in a searing flash of lightning that surges between the clouds and the ground along a pathway only a few millimeters wide. The air is heated to a blinding 54,000°F, five times as hot as the surface of the Sun.

▽ When lightning strikes, a "leader stroke" first jumps from cloud-base to ground. This creates a conducting pathway for the *upward* surge of the main discharge.

Heated by this surge of energy, the air expands violently – at the speed of sound – and it is this shock wave that we hear as the clap of thunder. If the storm is overhead, we hear the thunder as a deafening bang. If it is some distance away, the thunder may crash and rumble for several seconds as its echoes bounce back and forth between the clouds and the ground, or between nearby hills. The time difference between the flash and the bang gives a measure of how far away a storm is: one kilometer for every three seconds, or one mile for every five seconds.

The effects of a lightning strike are dramatic. Anything hit by the bolt will be heated through thousands of degrees in a split second. Most substances simply vaporize. Many explode. Yet miraculously there are many cases of people being hit – and walking away unscathed.

△ Ball lightning is still a mystery to scientists. The discharge appears like a glowing ball about the size of a football, which drifts about in the air with an erratic movement. Eventually it fades away, or disappears with a pop like a bursting bubble, or – fortunately less common – it may disappear in a violent explosion.

Observing the weather

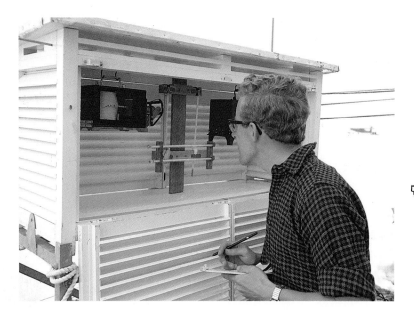

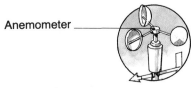

Anemometer

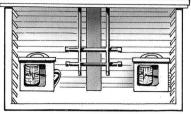

Before weather forecasters can even begin to predict what the weather will do tomorrow, they need to know precisely what is happening today. Information about air temperatures, pressures, humidity, wind speeds and cloud formations can provide a picture of how the atmosphere is behaving – and what it is most likely to do next.

Readings are taken with a standard set of instruments. They are kept in a special outdoor housing called a Stevenson screen, which is open to the air but protected from Sun and rain.

Temperature is given by a pair of vertical thermometers. One gives a straightforward air temperature. The other has wet muslin wrapped around the bulb. If the **humidity** – the amount of moisture in the air – is less than 100 percent, water **evaporates** from the muslin and lowers the thermometer reading. The humidity can then be calculated from the difference between the readings of the "wet" and "dry" thermometers.

△ In addition to wet and dry thermometers, a Stevenson screen houses two horizontally mounted thermometers that record the maximum and minimum temperatures since the last observation. It also houses a **thermograph**, which records temperature, and a **hygrograph**, which records humidity. Both make continuous records on paper charts mounted on motor-driven drums.

Outside the screen, an **anemometer** records the wind speed and direction. The instrument has a weather vane, and three cups that spin round in the wind. Readings are relayed to automatic recorders in the **meteorologist's** office. Other outdoor instruments record the hours of sunshine, and the amount of rain that falls. Indoors, a **barometer** measures the air pressure.

These measurements are taken every three hours, day and night, year in year out. From this mass of information the meteorologists can obtain a picture of the way the various air masses are behaving, the pattern of Highs and Lows, and the speed and direction of approaching weather systems. In high-risk areas they can provide warnings of gales or flooding.

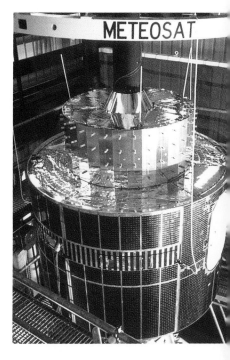

△Satellites like the European Space Agency's Meteosat are now widely used for weather research and forecasting. From their high orbits, satellites can track and photograph entire weather systems.

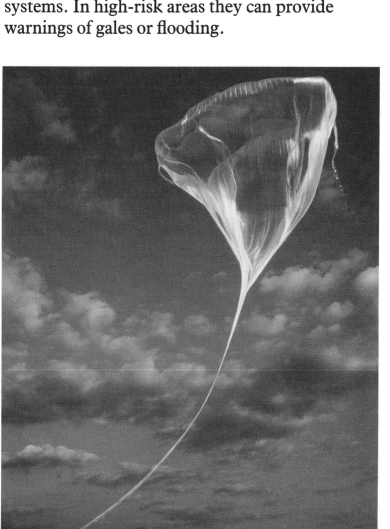

◁To learn more about the upper atmosphere, instrument packages are sent aloft by high-altitude balloon. This one – part of an American research program – was 180 m (600 ft) high at the launch. Initially these balloons are only partially filled, because at high altitude, where the pressure is very low, a small volume of gas will expand and fully inflate the balloon.

Weather forecasting

Weather forecasting has benefited enormously from the development of computers. Analyzing the mass of information from hundreds of weather stations used to be a long and painstaking task, but now much of the basic work can be done at high speed by machines. This allows the forecaster more time to concentrate on the skilled business of interpreting the information.

Satellite photographs are now beamed to the main forecasting centers, enabling scientists to watch the progress of a depression, hurricane or particularly severe snowstorm as it tracks across land and sea. Fresh pictures can arrive every 30 minutes, giving the forecaster a constantly updated view of the storm's progress – and clues about its likely future behavior.

△ A scene that would have been unimaginable to a weather forecaster of 50 years ago – a meteorologist surrounded by computer terminals and monitors. Today, for the first time since forecasting began, all the weather station readings can be processed before the next batch comes in. Forecasts involving 800,000 million separate calculations can be done in about 1 second!

▷ A forecaster at Redwood City Weather Station in California updates one of his weather charts.

Electronics have also greatly improved the means of spreading the latest forecasts to those who need them. The captain of a ship, for example, can receive the latest weather map by radio and see it printed out immediately on a facsimile machine. Dangerous storm areas can be avoided, while simply being able to sail with a following wind rather than a headwind can save thousands of dollars worth of fuel. Aircraft, too, need up-to-the-minute information, especially if there are thunderstorms along route.

Fishermen, farmers, traffic police and power supply engineers are just some of the other specialists who need fast, accurate weather information. For most of us, the weather report is something we simply take for granted.

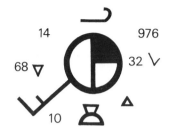

△ The three-hourly report from any weather station can be plotted on a chart using codes and symbols. Number codes are used for pressures, temperatures and visibility. Picture symbols at top and bottom indicate cloud types, and the "flag" shows the wind speed and direction.

Can we change the weather?

The scientist's dream of controlling the weather is likely to remain a dream. The forces involved are simply too great to be controlled.

However, new technology and new forecasting methods are constantly making the forecasters' predictions more accurate. And even if we cannot control the weather on a large scale, we can already alter it on a small scale. One method is called cloud seeding. It involves scattering crystals of silver iodide, or dry ice (frozen carbon dioxide), on to clouds to trigger off rainfall. As a means of producing rain it is unpredictable, but making a large cloud formation shed its water greatly reduces its energy – so this method could provide a means of weakening hurricanes or of making them change course away from cities.

△ The level of atmospheric **pollution** continues to grow in many countries, despite anti-pollution laws. Once released into the air, the poisons and acids are swept along in the moving airstreams and can affect areas hundreds of kilometers away.

More important is that we may be changing the atmosphere accidentally. Industries pour sulfur dioxide and nitrogen oxides into the air. These chemicals combine with water and fall as dilute acids, killing trees and wildlife.

Other chemicals, called CFCs, which are mixtures of carbon, chlorine, and fluorine are used in such items as refrigerators and spray cans. They are damaging a layer of ozone gas in the stratosphere. This layer blocks out most of the burning ultraviolet radiation that comes from the sun. "Ozone holes" caused by CFCs were discovered in the 1980s. If they continue to grow, more ultraviolet radiation will reach the Earth's surface.

Also, when forests are burned, the carbon dioxide in the atmosphere increases. This gas holds in the Earth's warmth, causing a "greenhouse effect," which might change world climates.

▽ The sad sight of acid rain damage in Austria. When the forest is gone, so too are its birds and insects, its squirrels, foxes, deer and wild boar. Finally, even the forest's value as a tourist attraction will be lost.

△ The natural water cycle is very easily polluted by industrial gases. These are absorbed by water in the atmosphere, and this produces acid which later falls as acid rain. Large areas of forest and many lakes have already been damaged in this way.

Glossary

Atmosphere The thin layer of gases surrounding the Earth. Most of the atmosphere is compressed into a layer 6 miles (10 km) thick near the poles, deepening over the equator to about 10 miles (16 km).

Atmosphere The thin layer of gases surrounding the Earth. Most of the atmosphere is compressed into a layer 10 km (6 miles) thick at the equator, thickening to 20 km (12 miles) in the polar regions.

Aurora Lights in the sky caused by electrically charged particles from the Sun hitting atoms of the atmosphere. The northern lights are called Aurora borealis; the southern ones Aurora australis.

Barometer An instrument for measuring atmospheric pressure.

Condense Turn from a gas or vapor into a liquid. Water in your breath will condense when you breathe on a cold window pane.

Depression A low-pressure weather system, often with cold weather, winds and rain and snow.

Dew point The temperature at which water vapor in the air condenses into drops of liquid water.

Drizzle Very fine rain consisting of drops less than 0.5 mm in diameter. This kind of rain falls from very thin layer cloud.

Evaporate Change from a liquid into a gas or vapor. The opposite of condense. A puddle dries up because the water has evaporated into the air.

Front The boundary that separates two large air masses of different temperature. A warm front marks the edge of an approaching mass of warm air. A cold front marks approaching cold air.

Gravity The invisible force that pulls a small light object toward a big heavy one. The Sun's gravity holds the Earth in its orbit. Earth's gravity keeps us on the surface and holds the atmosphere in place.

Humidity A measure of the amount of water in the air. It is usually given as a percentage of the maximum amount of water the air could hold at the same temperature: then it is called relative humidity.

Hygrograph An instrument for measuring and recording the humidity of the air.

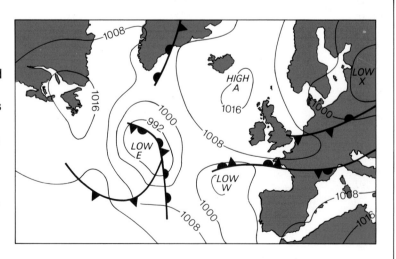

▷This Atlantic weather chart shows a typical pattern of Highs and Lows. High A is controlling the weather in the British Isles. Its clockwise wind circulation is pulling cold air in from Europe. The east coast is cloudy and bright, but in the west, where the wind makes a longer sea crossing, there is thicker cloud, rain and strong winds.

In the next few days, High A and Low W drifted south-east, while Low E pushed its way toward Scotland.

Magnetic field The Earth behaves as if it has a magnet running through it from pole to pole. The lines of force are concentrated at the poles, and this is where protons and electrons from the Sun become trapped, producing auroras.

Meteorologist A scientist who studies the weather.

Molecule The smallest particle of a substance that can exist. A molecule of water, for example, consists of one atom of oxygen and two atoms of hydrogen.

Monsoon The season of very heavy rain that occurs in India and South Asia. During the monsoon the normal winds, and some ocean currents, reverse their directions.

Photochemical smog A kind of smog that is caused by the chemical action of sunlight on the exhaust gases from motor vehicles.

Pollution Anything that fouls or spoils the environment, such as smoke, rubbish dumped in the countryside, or chemicals tipped into rivers or the sea.

Precipitation General name for water in any form falling from clouds. It includes rain, drizzle, hail, as well as snow and sleet.

Rain Liquid water droplets falling from clouds. Raindrops vary from less than a millimeter to about 5 mm in diameter.

Reflection Light bouncing back from any surface – the surface of the sea, a mirror, clean snow, or the inside of a single raindrop.

Refraction The bending of a light ray when it passes out of one transparent substance into another.

Saturated When air is saturated with water vapor, its relative humidity is 100 per cent and any extra vapor will condense as cloud, mist or fog.

Sleet A mixture of rain, snow and half-melted snow.

Static electricity Electricity occurs in two forms: in current electricity the charge is in motion. In static electricity the charge remains in one place.

Supercooled A gas or liquid is supercooled when it has been cooled *below* its normal freezing point but has not become solid.

Temperate The word means moderate, and is used to describe the climatic zone between the warm tropics and the very cold polar regions.

Thermograph An instrument for measuring and recording temperature. It consists of strips of two different metals, fixed together. When they are warmed or cooled they expand and contract at different rates and so the strip tries to curl and uncurl. This movement is linked to a pen tracing a record on a revolving drum.

Wavelength Light is just one kind of radiation, along with radio waves, heat, ultraviolet and many others.

White light The light we get from the Sun is a mixture of light of all colors. We call it "white" light, but it can be split into the rainbow colors of the spectrum by passing it through water drops or glass lenses.

Day

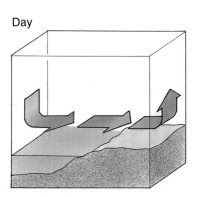

Night

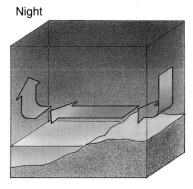

◁**Land and sea breezes** During the day, land warms up more quickly than the sea. The air above it rises and is replaced by cool air drawn in from over the sea. This gives the refreshing sea breeze. At night, the land cools faster than the sea and the breeze blows in the opposite direction.

Index

PRINTED IN BELGIUM BY

proost
INTERNATIONAL BOOK PRODUCTION